INFOGRAPHIC TOP 10

RECORD-BREAKING EARTH & SPACE

Jon Richards and Ed Simkins

WAYLAND

CONTENTS

pages 4–5
See what is inside a volcano and discover how violent a volcanic eruption can be.

pages 10–11
Discover why conditions on our planet are just right for life to exist.

WELCOME!

From the biggest to the closest and from the driest to the fastest, this book looks at the amazing record-breakers in the Universe. It uses stunning icons, graphics and visualisations to show you how these amazing planets, stars, comets and asteroids are true galactic greats.

pages 22–23
Find out about the planets that exist outside the Solar System and measure how big they are.

pages 26–27
Weigh how much Moon rock was brought back by the Apollo missions.

CRACKED SURFACE

<— · · · · · · · · · · · · · · · · ·—>

The surface of Earth is cracked like the shell of an egg into various, uneven and jagged tectonic plates. These move around slowly, bashing into each other and creating shattering earthquakes, spouting volcanoes and towering mountains.

What's inside a volcano

A volcano is an opening in the crust where molten rock, ash, steam and gases escape from the planet's interior.

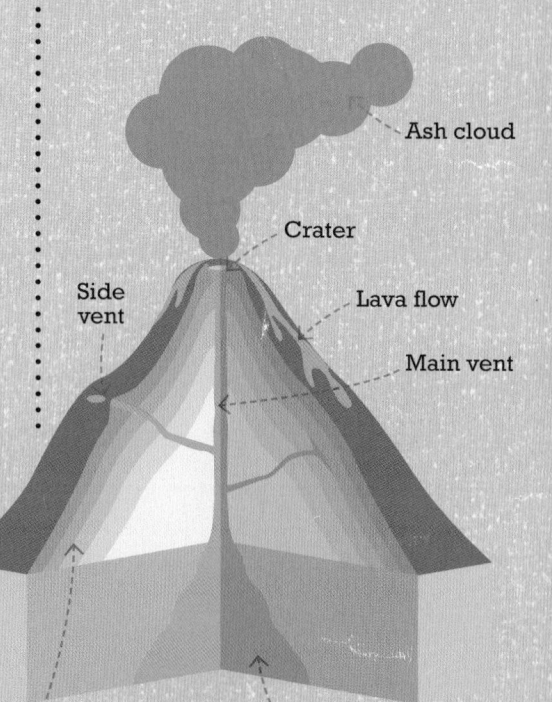

Ash cloud

Crater

Side vent

Lava flow

Main vent

Cone built up from ash and lava from previous eruptions

Magma chamber

Most active volcano

The most active volcano on the planet is **Kilauea** in **Hawaii**. It has been erupting continuously since 1983 and lava erupts from it at a rate of 5 cubic metres every second.

8 mins 20 sec

That's fast enough to fill an Olympic swimming pool in...

Lava reaches 1,250°C – hot enough to melt gold.

Pyroclastic flows are clouds of scorching rock and gas that pour out of a volcano. They typically move at speeds of 80 km/h, but the fastest can travel at **480 km/h**, which is **1.5 times faster** than a Formula One car.

How mountains are formed

Everest is the tallest mountain on Earth and is **8,848 m** high. It was created by two tectonic plates crashing into each other, forming the towering **Himalayas**.

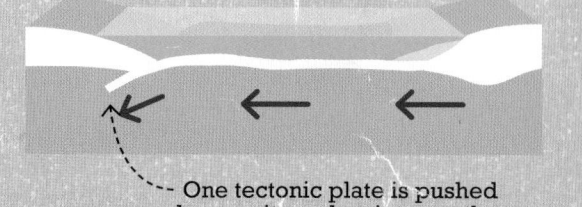

One tectonic plate is pushed down as it crashes into another.

90%
of volcanoes are found around the Pacific Ring of Fire.

Volcanoes can send an ash cloud up to an altitude of 30 km.

That's 3.5 times the height of Everest.

LARGEST TECTONIC PLATES

1. **Pacific – 103,300,000 sq km**
2. **North America – 75,900,000 sq km**
3. **Eurasia – 67,800,000 sq km**
4. **Africa – 61,300,000 sq km**
5. **Antarctica – 60,900,000 sq km**
6. **Australia – 47,000,000 sq km**
7. **South America 43,600,000 sq km**
8. **Somalia – 16,700,000 sq km**
9. **Nazca – 15,600,000 sq km**
10. **India – 11,900,000 sq km**

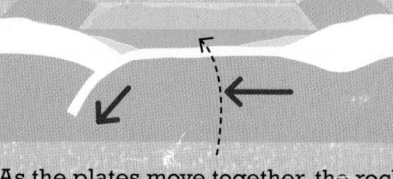

As the plates move together, the rock between them starts to clump up.

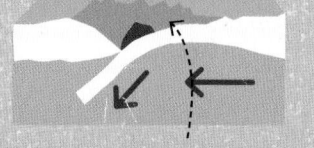

Rock is pushed up between the plates, creating mountains.

Growing Himalayas

The Himalayas are currently growing at a rate of about 1 cm per year.

DRY PLANET

<‹ ···· ›>

Deserts are the driest places on the planet, receiving less than 25 cm of precipitation a year. They cover about one-third of the land and range in habitat from the scorching wastes of the Sahara in Africa to the frozen realm of Antarctica.

Ice desert

Antarctica is the largest desert in the world (bigger than the continental USA). It is actually covered with water, but that is all **frozen**.

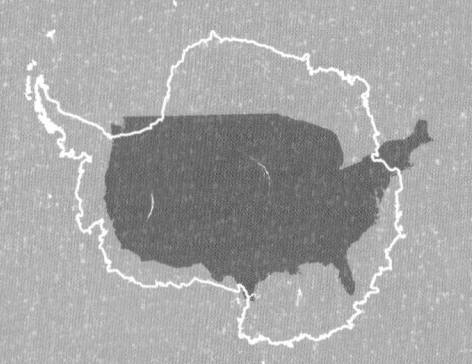

The **average thickness** of the ice is more than 1.6 km. That's twice the height of the **Burj Khalifa**, the world's tallest building.

Atacama Desert

The **Atacama Desert** in Chile is a rain shadow desert and the driest place on the planet. Its average rainfall is just 0.1 mm per year – that's just **1 cm of rain every 100 years.**

If the ice caps melted the sea level would rise **60m**...

Flooded

... and the world's coastlines would look like this.

The **hottest** and **coldest** temperatures recorded on Earth were both measured in **deserts**.

–89.2°C	–12.3°C	–18°C	0°C	15°C	37°C	56.7°C
Vostok Station, Antarctica	Highest temperature recorded at the South Pole	Optimum temperature for a freezer	Freezing point of water	Average temperature of Earth	Body temperature	Furnace Creek, Death Valley, California

❄ Lowest

☀ Highest

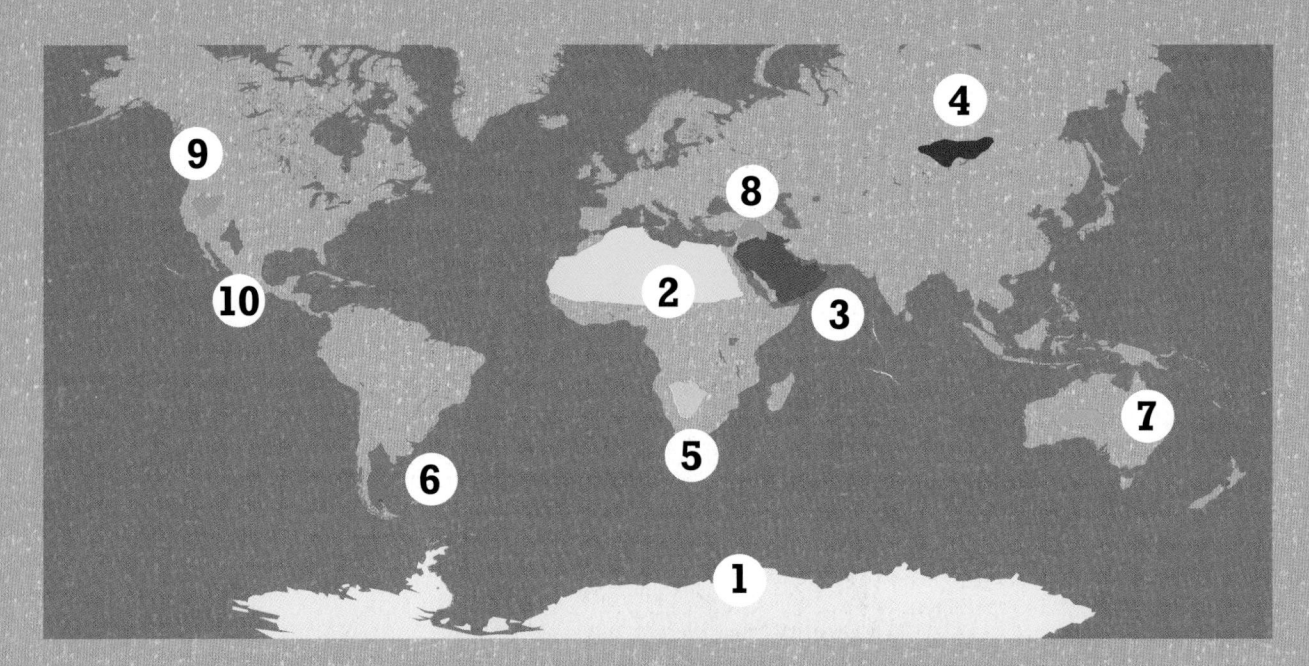

LARGEST DESERTS IN THE WORLD

1. **Antarctica – 14.2 million sq km**
2. Sahara – 8.6 million sq km
3. **Arabian Desert – 2.3 million sq km**
4. Gobi Desert – 1.3 million sq km
5. **Kalahari Desert – 930,000 sq km**
6. Patagonian Desert – 673,000 sq km
7. **Great Victoria Desert – 647,000 sq km**
8. Syrian desert – 518,000 sq km
9. **Great Basin Desert – 492,000 sq km**
10. Chihuahuan Desert – 282,000 sq km

How a rain shadow desert forms

Rain

Wind

Dry air

Evaporation

Mountain

Water vapour is picked up from the ocean to create moist air. This air is pushed up by a mountain range, where the water falls as rain. This leaves **dry air** to pass over to the other side of the mountains, creating the very dry conditions that form rain shadow deserts.

LIFE ON EARTH

‹···›

Earth is the only place in the Solar System where life has been found (so far). It is the perfect distance from the Sun to be the right temperature for liquid water, which is vital for life, to exist.

(1)

The **forested area** of Russia is about the same size as the **entire country** of Brazil.

(2)

(3)

(4)

A single tree can absorb about **22 kg** of carbon dioxide in a year and produce enough oxygen for two people.

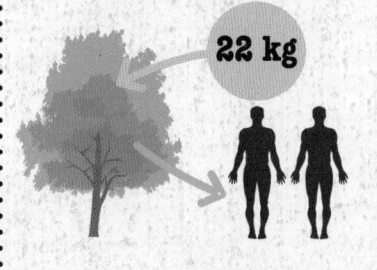

22 kg

0.84 kg

An average adult human uses about 0.84 kg of oxygen every day.

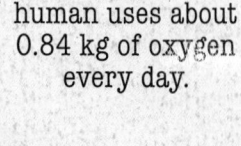

1 kg

The average human exhales just over 1 kg of carbon dioxide every day.

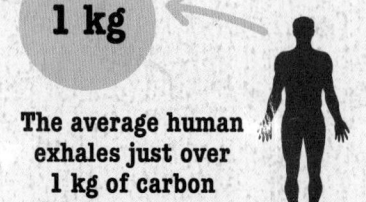

COUNTRIES WITH THE LARGEST COMBINED FOREST AREA

1. **Russia – 8.5 million sq km**
2. Brazil – 5.4 million sq km
3. **Canada – 2.4 million sq km**
4. USA – 2.3 million sq km
5. **China – 1.6 million sq km**
6. Australia – 1.5 million sq km
7. **Dem Rep of Congo – 1.4 million sq km**
8. Indonesia – 1 million sq km
9. **Angola – 698,000 sq km**
10. Peru – 652,000 sq km

Biomass facts

The combined mass of living things is called biomass. These figures show the creatures with some of the greatest biomass.

Humans 350 million tonnes
Seven billion people weighing an average of 50 kg each.

Termites 445 million tonnes
A single termite nest can be home to millions of individual termites.

Atlantic Krill 379 million tonnes
Trillions of these tiny creatures swarm together providing food for other marine animals.

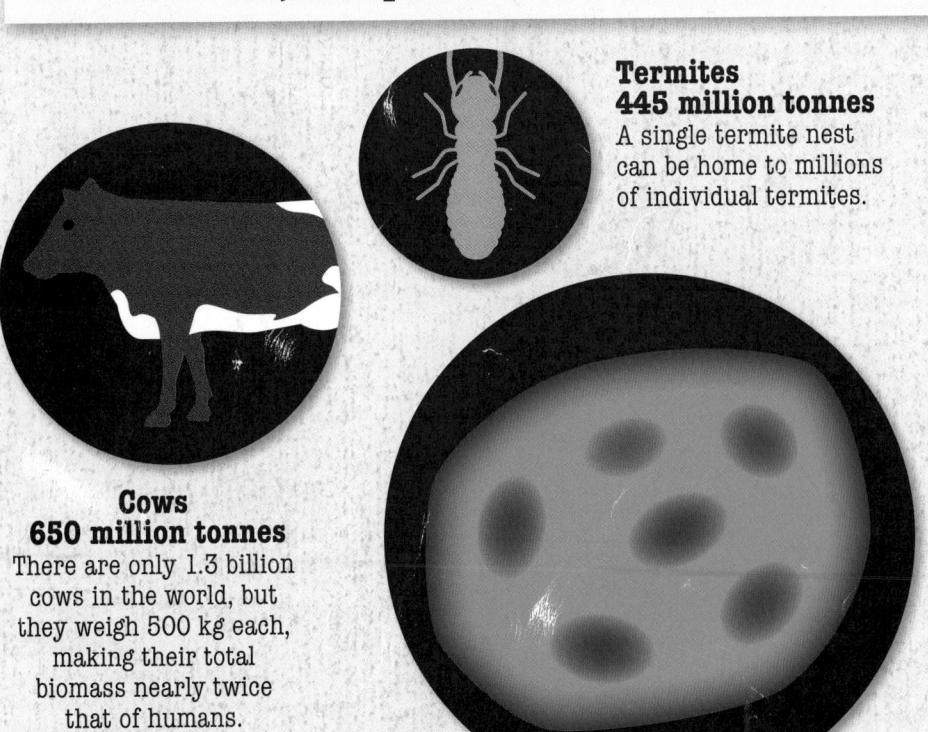

Cows 650 million tonnes
There are only 1.3 billion cows in the world, but they weigh 500 kg each, making their total biomass nearly twice that of humans.

Cyanobacteria 1 billion tonnes
Some of the smallest living things on the planet, make up the greatest amount of biomass.

Blue Whales 0.5 million tonnes
In contrast, the total biomass of the largest animal to have ever lived is just 0.5 million tonnes.

5 6 7 8 9 10

THE SOLAR SYSTEM

The family of planets, dwarf planets and small objects, such as asteroids, is called the Solar System. At its centre is a ball of burning gas; the Sun. So what are the largest objects in the Solar System?

6 Earth
Earth is the third planet from the Sun and it has one natural satellite the Moon.
12,742 km

7 Venus
The second planet from the Sun has an atmosphere that's so thick that we cannot see the planet's surface.
12,104 km

8 Mars
Mars is called the red planet because its surface contains a lot of iron oxide, or rust.
6,780 km

9 Ganymede
Orbiting Jupiter, Ganymede is the largest moon in the Solar System and bigger than the planet Mercury.
5,268 km

10 Titan
Titan is Saturn's largest moon and its surface has seas, lakes and rivers of methane and ethane.
5,152 km

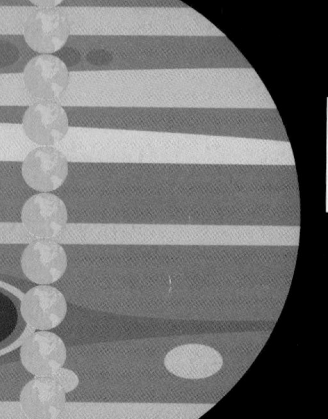

Giant planet

Jupiter has about 1,320 times the volume of Earth, its **diameter** is 11 times that of Earth and it has a surface area that is 120 times **bigger**.

However, it is only 317 times Earth's mass, because its density is one-quarter that of our planet.

Goldilocks Zone

If a planet is too close to the Sun, then conditions are **too hot** for life to exist. Too far away, and conditions are **too cold**. In between is a region called the Goldilocks Zone, where conditions are **just right** for life.

Mars
Earth
Venus
too hot
Sun
Mercury
Goldilocks zone
too cold

4 Uranus

This planet is a bright blue colour because its atmosphere contains a lot of methane.

50,724 km

5 Neptune

This planet is almost the same size as Uranus, and it takes nearly 165 years to orbit the Sun.

49,244 km

3 Saturn

Saturn is surrounded by a bright ring system, which is made up of pieces of ice and rock.

116,464 km

2 Jupiter

The largest planet in the Solar System, Jupiter is the fifth planet from the Sun.

142,984 km

Sun facts

1 Sun

The Sun produces light and heat by fusing together hydrogen atoms, which releases energy.

1,391,016 km

It makes up 99.8% of the entire Solar System's mass. It will continue to shine for 5.5 billion years, before expanding beyond Earth's orbit and then shrinking to form a tiny white dwarf star.

IN A SPIN

Every planet spins around on its axis, creating periods of day and night. Jupiter is the fastest spinning planet in the Solar System, and its day only lasts for 9.8 Earth hours.

PLANETS AND DWARF PLANETS WITH THE LONGEST DAYS (EARTH TIME)

1. **Venus – 245 days 0 hours 25 minutes 55 seconds**
2. Mercury – 58 days 15 hours 30 minutes 14 seconds
3. **Sun – 25 days 9 hours 7 minutes 26 seconds**
4. Pluto – 6 days 9 hours 17 minutes 17 seconds
5. **Eris – 1 day 1 hour 53 minutes 46 seconds**
6. Mars – 24 hours 37 minutes 26 seconds
7. **Earth – 23 hours 56 minutes 41 seconds**
8. Makemake – 22 hours 29 minutes 17 seconds
9. **Uranus – 17 hours 13 minutes 55 seconds**
10. Neptune – 16 hours 6 minutes 4 seconds

Lengths of the seasons

Mars
7 months

Earth
90–93 days

Venus
55–58 days

Jupiter
3 years

Saturn
7 years

Uranus
20 years

The planets move around the Sun in paths called **orbits**. Because the planets are **tilted**, different parts of each planet point towards the Sun at different parts of these orbits, creating the **seasons**. The length of the planets' seasons varies greatly depending on their **tilt** and the **length** of their orbit.

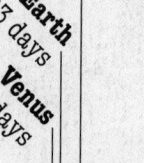

Changing shape

Jupiter's fast spin actually **squashes** the planet slightly, creating a shape called an oblate spheroid. It is more than **4,500 km wider** than it is **tall**.

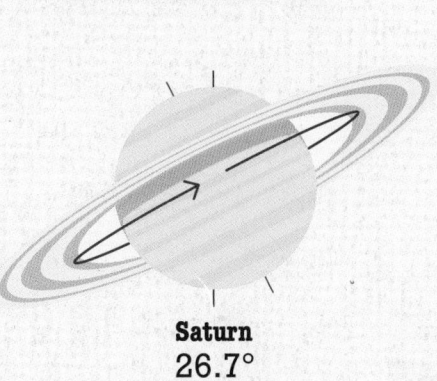

138,346.5 km

142,984 km

Axial tilt

The objects that make up the Solar System spin around at different angles, known as the **axial tilt**. The images here show the planets in the Solar System with the greatest axial tilt.

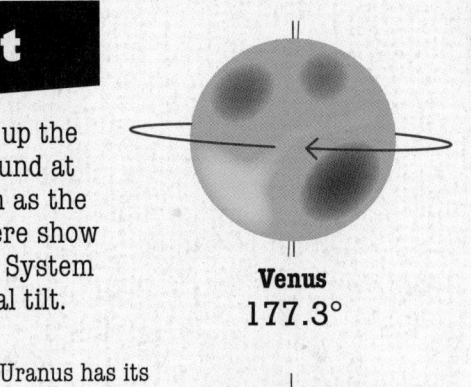

Venus
177.3°

Venus

The planet Venus actually spins in the **opposite direction** to the other planets – this is known as **retrograde spin**. If Earth rotated in the same direction as Venus, then the Sun would rise in the west and set in the east.

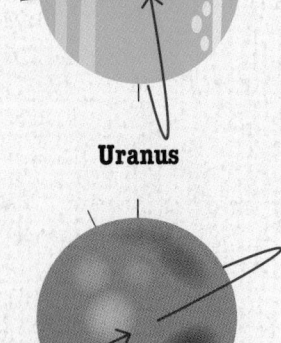

Uranus has its axis at an angle of 98° and spins on its side.

Uranus

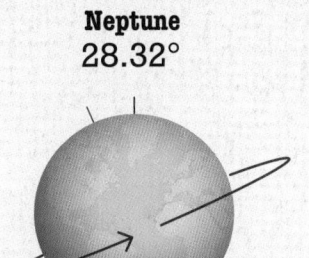

Neptune
28.32°

Saturn
26.7°

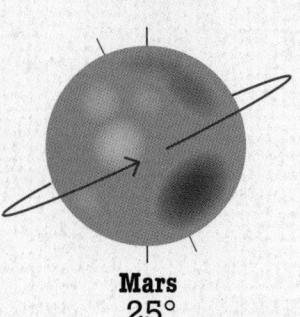

Mars
25°

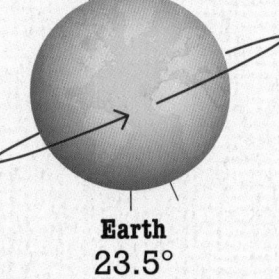

Earth
23.5°

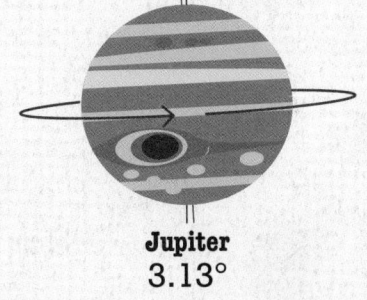

Jupiter
3.13°

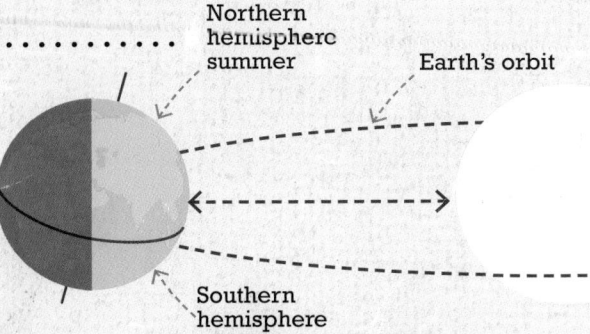

Northern hemisphere summer

Earth's orbit

Northern hemisphere winter

Southern hemisphere winter

Southern hemisphere summer

Neptune 40 years

ON THE SURFACE

← · · · · · · · · · · · · · · · →

The four planets closest to the Sun have rocky surfaces that are covered with towering peaks, huge chasms and the scars of impacts from asteroids and comets.

Olympus Mons

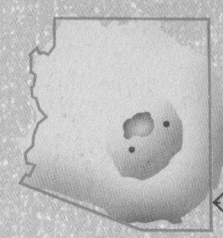

This Martian volcano covers the same area as Arizona, USA.

←- - - - Arizona

Its peak is **three times** higher than Everest.

The six craters (calderas) at the summit are about 85 km wide – nearly twice the size of Greater London, UK, which is 48 km wide.

←- Greater London

Six craters

Valles Marineris

This huge canyon on Mars is up to 10 km deep. That's about 10 times the depth of the Grand Canyon.

It stretches around 20 per cent of the whole of **Mars**, and would stretch across **North America**.

The huge peak of Pavonis Mons on Mars measures 375 km across.

When measured from the sea floor, Mauna Kea is the tallest mountain on Earth and one of five volcanoes that make up the island of Hawaii, USA.

② ④ ⑥ ⑦ 10

TALLEST MOUNTAINS IN THE SOLAR SYSTEM (HEIGHT)

1. **Olympus Mons (Mars) – 24.8 km**
2. Rheasilvia Mons (Vesta) – 21.1 km
3. **Equatorial Ridge (Iapetus) – 19.8 km**
4. Ascraeus Mons (Mars) – 18.1 km
5. **Boösaule Montes (Io) – 17.4 km**
6. Arsia Mons (Mars) – 15.8 km
7. **Pavonis Mons (Mars) – 13.9 km**
8. Elysium Mons (Mars) – 12.5 km
9. **Maxwell Montes (Venus) – 10.9 km**
10. Mauna Kea (Earth) – 9.1 km

A 100-km wide asteroid hit Mercury about 4 billion years ago, creating a huge crater called the Caloris Basin. This is 1,550 km wide and could contain the state of Texas, USA.

Olympus Mons is surrounded by a cliff that is about 10 km high.

Boösaule Montes is found on Jupiter's moon, Io, the most volcanically active body in the Solar System.

Maxwell Montes is a mountain range that is about 850 km long and 700 km wide.

DEEP IMPACT

The Solar System is not a safe place! Millions of pieces of rock and ice are flying around at enormous speeds. Sometimes, they slam into planets with devastating results.

Yucatán impact

About **66 million years ago,** an object about **10 km** across hit the Earth with the force of around **one billion atomic bombs.**

10 km

The object was travelling at a speed of nearly **30 km a second.** That's more than 150 times faster that a **jet airliner.**

Crater

Gulf of Mexico

Yucatán Peninsula

Mexico

At the moment of impact, the asteroid created a **crater** that was **100 km** across and about **30 km** deep.

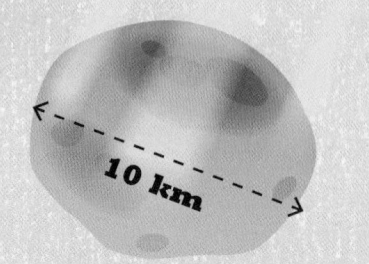

100 km

30 km

It's likely that the impact created an enormous **tsunami,** measuring **4–5 km** high – about 6.5 times the height of the **Burj Khalifa.**

4–5 km

The collision threw up so much **dust and pollution** that scientists believe it blocked out the Sun for up to **6 months,** leading to...

... acid rain, ...

... collapse of photosynthesis...

... and global temperature reduction.

This **change in conditions** was so great that it caused the **extinction** of the **dinosaurs.**

Shoemaker-Levy 9

In 1994, fragments from comet Shoemaker-Levy 9 slammed into Jupiter with incredible force. The pieces were travelling at 216,000 km/h.

The largest piece was about **3–4 km** wide and left a hole in its atmosphere **twice the size of Earth.**

Earth

Impact scars

BIGGEST CRATERS IN THE SOLAR SYSTEM (DIAMETER)

1. **Borealis Basin (Mars) – 8,500 km**
2. **Valhalla (Callisto) – 4,000 km**
3. **South Pole-Aitken Basin (Moon) – 2,500 km**
4. **Hellas Basin (Mars) – 2,100 km**
5. **Argyre Basin (Mars) – 1,800 km**
6. **Caloris Basin (Mercury) – 1,550 km**
7. **Isidis Planitia (Mars) – 1,500 km**
8. **Asgard (Callisto) – 1,400 km**
9. **Mare Imbrium (Moon) – 1,100 km**
10. **Turgis (Iapetus) – 580 km**

How the Moon was formed

About 4.6 billion years ago, an object the size of **Mars** slammed into **Earth**, creating a spray of debris that clumped together to form the **Moon**.

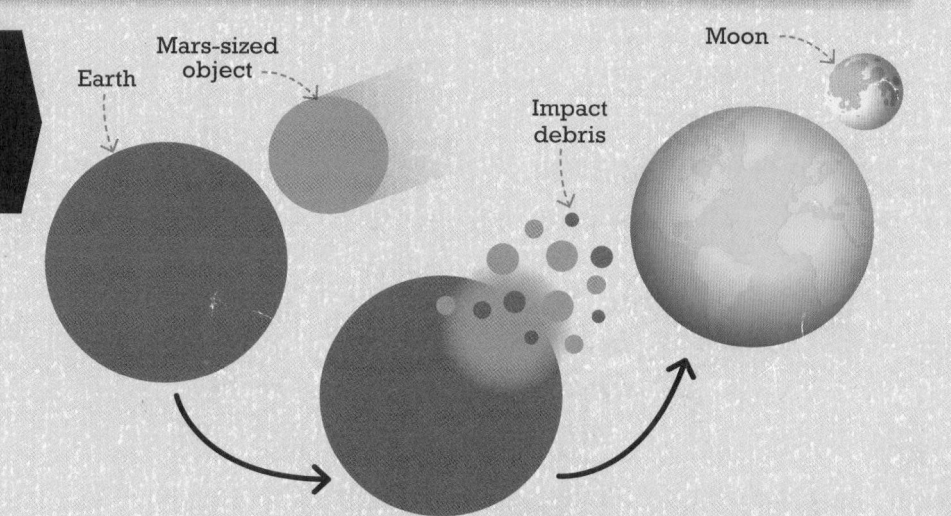

Earth — Mars-sized object — Impact debris — Moon

Chelyabinsk meteor

In 2013, a **20-m** wide piece of rock with a mass of **10,000 tonnes** entered Earth's atmosphere and exploded in the air over Russia.
The explosion injured 1,200 people.
It had a force equivalent to about
500 kilotonnes of TNT – nearly **30 times** the force of the atomic bomb dropped on Hiroshima.

SURFACE CONDITIONS

From scorching worlds to freezing globes, conditions on the Solar System's planets and minor planets vary greatly. On some planets, the gravity is so great that you would struggle to move, while on others it is so small that you could leap unbelievably high.

Boiling point of mercury **357°C**

Melting point of lead **327°C**

450°C **400°C** **350°C** **300°C** **250°C** **200°C** **150°C**

Boiling point of sulphur **445°C**

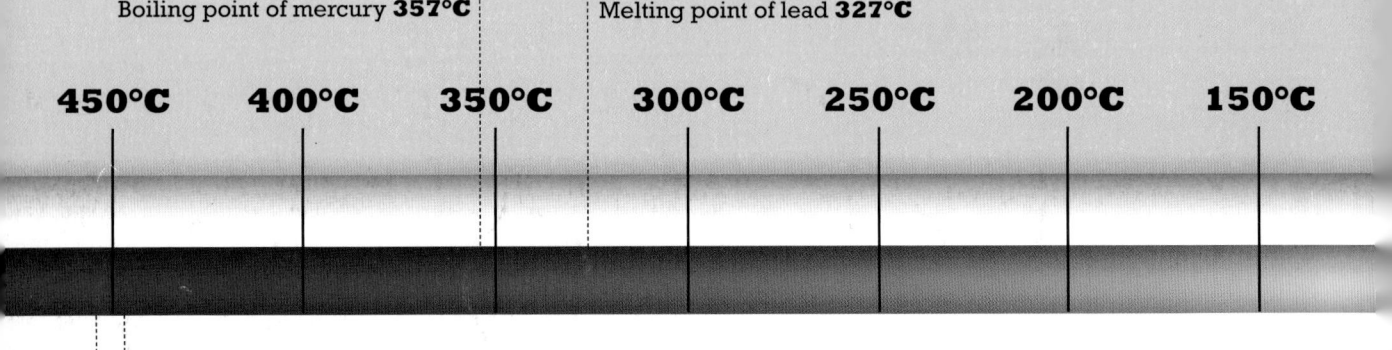

Venus

1

Venus's thick atmosphere is made up almost entirely of carbon dioxide. This acts like an enormous greenhouse, trapping heat and warming the planet to scorching temperatures.

What would you weigh?

How the weight of a 75-kg person would vary on different bodies in the Solar System.

Pluto	Moon	Mars	Mercury	Uranus	Venus	Earth	Saturn	Neptune	Jupiter
5 kg	12.4 kg	28.2 kg	28.3kg	66.6 kg	68 kg	75 kg	79.8 kg	84.3 kg	177.3 kg
(x0.06)	(x0.17)	(x0.38)	(x0.38)	(x0.89)	(x0.9)	(x1)	(x1.06)	(x1.12)	(x2.36)

Pluto

The gravity on Pluto, a dwarf planet, is only about 0.06 of that on Earth. A person who could make a 3-m slam dunk in basketball would be able to leap up to a height of 45 m on Pluto!

Highest temperature recorded on Earth **56.7°C**

1. **Venus 462°C**
2. **Earth 15°C**
=3. **Mars -63°C**
=3. **Mercury -63°C**
5. **Vesta -95.5°C**
6. **Ceres -105°C**
7. **Jupiter -145°C**
8. **Saturn -175°C**
9. **Neptune -218°C**
10. **Uranus -224°C**

Freezing point of water

50°C   **0°C**   **-50°C**   **-100°C**   **-150°C**   **-200°C**   **-250°C**

Human body temperature **37°C**

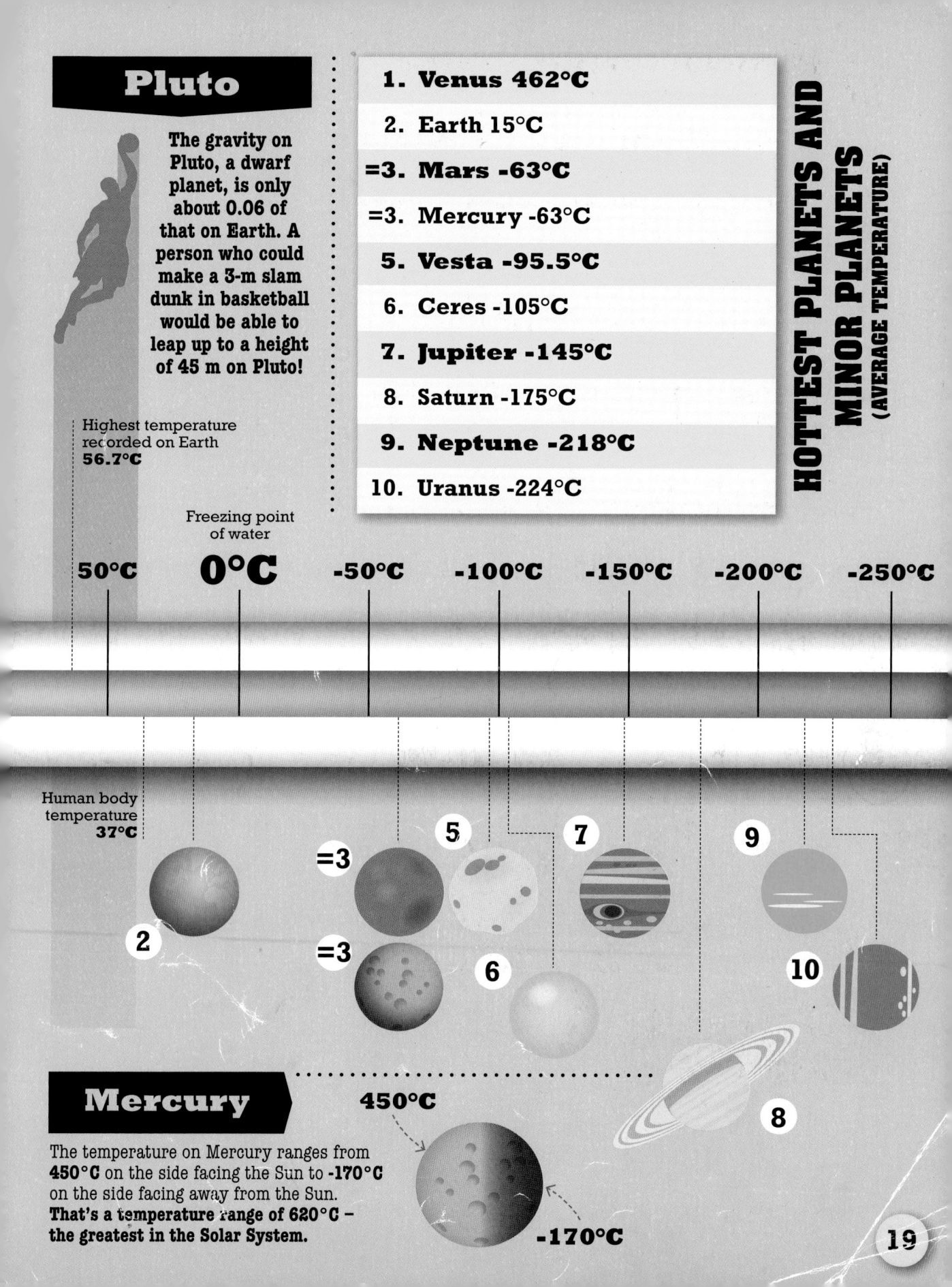

Mercury

The temperature on Mercury ranges from **450°C** on the side facing the Sun to **-170°C** on the side facing away from the Sun. **That's a temperature range of 620°C – the greatest in the Solar System.**

450°C

-170°C

SMALL BODIES

<——————————————————————>

Comets and asteroids may be small compared with the planets, but they can cause spectacular events, including glowing comet tails and shooting stars. The Solar System is populated with millions of these small bodies.

The Moon

1

2

3

4

5

6

7

8

9

10

Dwarf planet

The largest object in the Asteroid Belt is called **Ceres**. It has a diameter of **950 km** and was first spotted in 1801. It was initially classified as an **asteroid**, but in 2006, it was re-classified as a **dwarf planet**. A dwarf planet is an object that **orbits** the Sun, is **roughly** round in shape, but hasn't cleared its orbit of **other objects**.

On its own, Ceres accounts for 25 per cent of the Asteroid Belt's total mass.

LARGEST ASTEROIDS (DIAMETER)

1. 2 Pallas – 545 km
2. 4 Vesta – 530 km
3. 10 Hygiea – 407 km
4. 511 Davida – 326 km
5. 704 Interamnia – 316 km
6. 52 Europa – 302 km
7. 87 Sylvia – 260 km
=8. 31 Euphrosyne – 255 km
=8. 15 Eunomia – 255 km
10. 16 Psyche – 253 km

Most asteroids are found in a zone between Mars and Jupiter known as the Asteroid Belt. Scientists believe that the belt has more than 750,000 asteroids that are larger than 1 km across.

Comet probe

In November 2014, the probe **Philae** landed on the 4-km-wide comet 67P/Churyumov-Gerasimenko after a journey of **6.4 billion km**.

Comet facts

Comet particles that are bigger than **2 mm** burn up at 1,600°C as they enter the atmosphere, creating **shooting stars**.

Actual size

2 mins

Comet particles stream out at speeds of **350 km** a second. That is quick enough to travel around Earth in **less the 2 minutes**.

Every day, about 300 tonnes of dust, much of it from comets, reaches Earth – about the weight of **1.5 blue whales**.

Comet tails

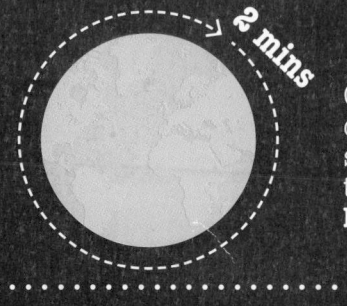

In 2007, the tail of Comet McNaught was measured at more than **224 million km long**.

That's about 1.5 times the distance from Earth to the Sun.

←----- 149,600,000 km -----→

DISTANT WORLDS

◄ ⋯⋯⋯⋯⋯⋯⋯⋯⋯⋯⋯⋯⋯⋯⋯⋯⋯⋯ ►

The exoplanet known as Kepler 42c completes an orbit around its star in just 4.3 hours.

Until recently, no-one had discovered planets outside our Solar System. However, in the last 25 years, hundreds of these exoplanets have been found circling other stars, and some of these are the largest planets ever discovered.

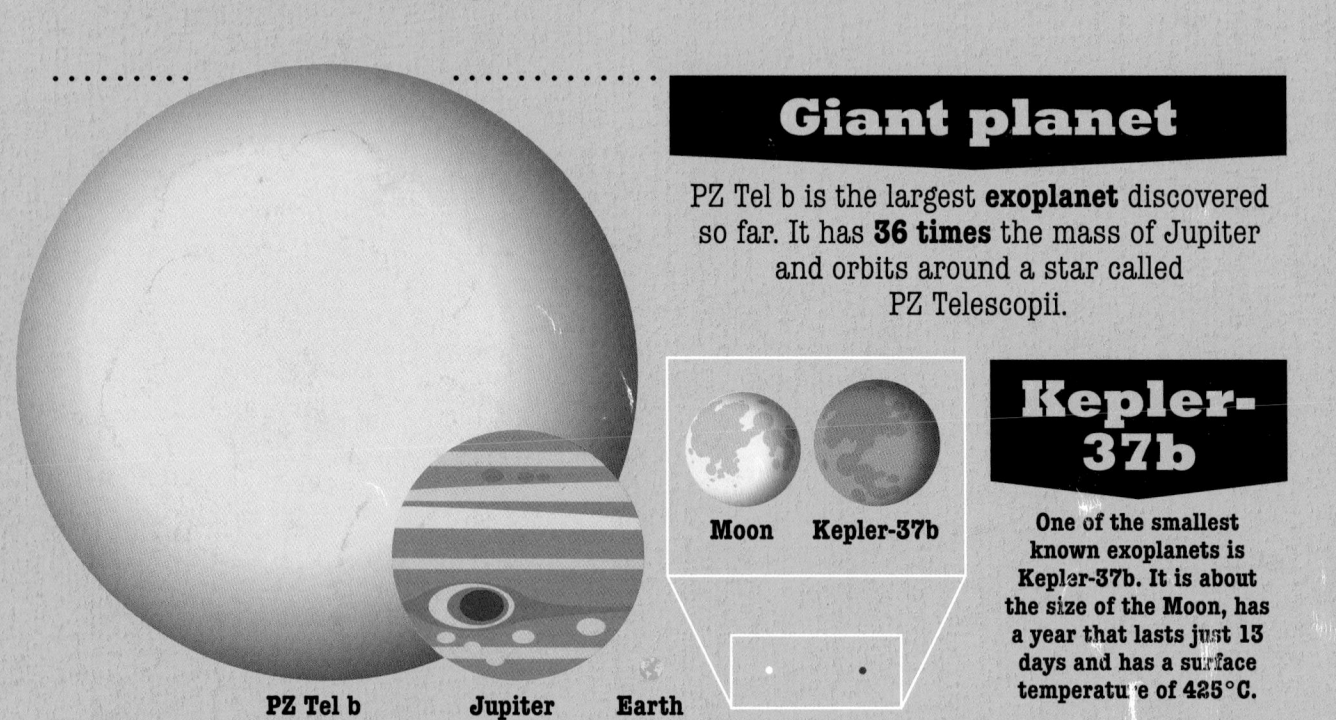

PZ Tel b   Jupiter   Earth

Moon   Kepler-37b

Giant planet

PZ Tel b is the largest **exoplanet** discovered so far. It has **36 times** the mass of Jupiter and orbits around a star called PZ Telescopii.

Kepler-37b

One of the smallest known exoplanets is Kepler-37b. It is about the size of the Moon, has a year that lasts just 13 days and has a surface temperature of 425°C.

PZ Tel b orbits its star at 18 times the distance from the Sun to Earth. Astronomers call this Sun–Earth distance an **astronomical unit** (AU).

PZ Telescopii and its giant planet lie about **175 light years** from Earth, and can be seen in the constellation Telescopium.

◄-------------------------- 18 AU

←⋯ 1 AU

Discovered in 2013, **Kepler-78b** is the same size as Earth, but it orbits its star in 8.5 hours and has a surface temperature of **2,826°C** – hot enough to melt iron!

Red-hot world

LARGEST EXOPLANETS
(TIMES EARTH)

1. **PZ Tel b – 27.1**

2. CT Cha b – 24.64

3. **HAT-P-32 b – 22.81**

4. WASP-17 b – 22.3

=5. **KOI-368.01 b – 20.5**

=5. WASP-76 – 20.5

7. **HAT-P33 b – 20.46**

8. GQ Lup b – 20.16

9. **WASP-78 b – 19.6**

10. WASP-12 b – 19.44

How many?

As many as one in five sun-like stars have an Earth-sized planet in the habitable Goldilocks Zone (see page 11). These planets may have the right conditions for life to exist.

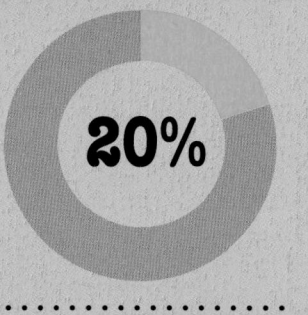

20%

How exoplanets are discovered

Exoplanets are usually too dim to be seen directly, so **astronomers** look out for the effects they might have on other objects, such as the light from the stars they orbit or from other objects that are **farther away**.

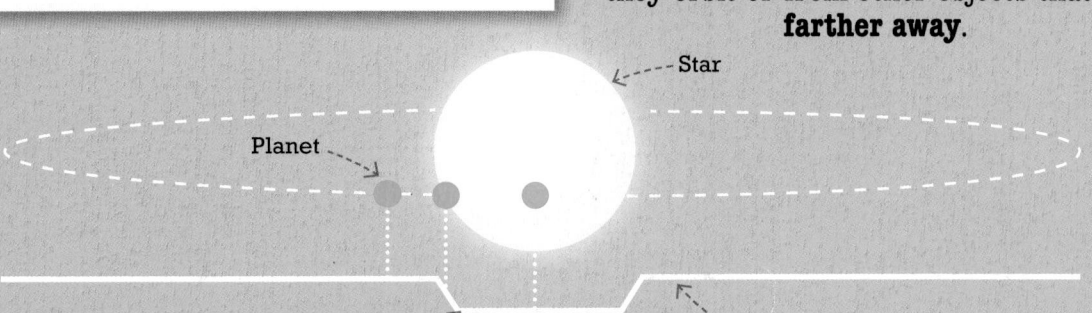

Star

Planet

Light dims

Light level

As the exoplanet travels **in front** of its star, it causes the star's light to **dim** slightly. Astronomers can use this method to calculate the **size** of the exoplanet.

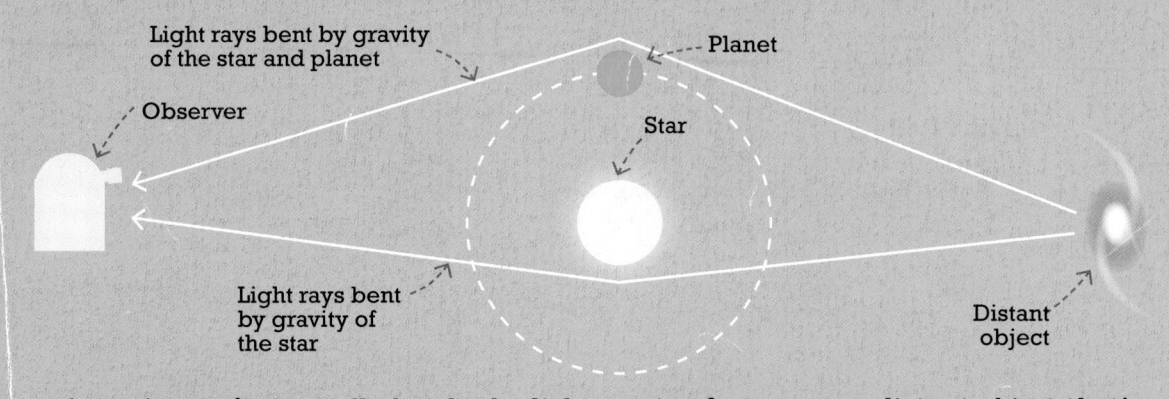

Light rays bent by gravity of the star and planet

Planet

Observer

Star

Light rays bent by gravity of the star

Distant object

A star's **gravity** actually bends the light coming from a more distant object that's far **behind** it. If that star has a planet orbiting it, then the gravity of the planet will cause the light to bend **even more,** distorting the image of the distant object.

STAR LIGHT, STAR BRIGHT

The Sun is one of billions of stars that form our galaxy, which is called the Milky Way. This chart shows the 10 stars and star systems that are closest to us and their distance in light years (ly).

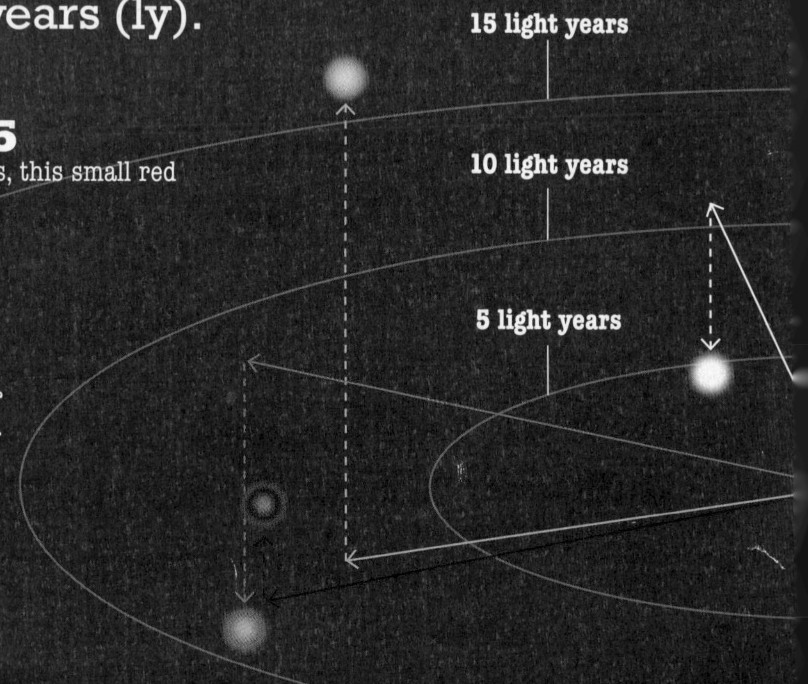

9 **Epsilon Eridani**
This orange dwarf star has a large, Jupiter-sized planet orbiting it.
10.52 ly

15 light years

10 light years

5 light years

4 **Lalande 21185**
Visible with the help of binoculars, this small red star is up to 10 billion years old.
8.29 ly

3 **Wolf 359**
This very dim red star was first seen in 1916.
7.78 ly

Dense stars

Neutron stars are so dense that a teaspoon full of their matter would have a mass of **1 billion tonnes** – equivalent to more than **1,500** fully laden supertankers.

5 **Sirius**
This system contains two stars, Sirius A and Sirius B. Sirius A is the brightest star in our night sky.
8.58 ly

1 **Alpha Centauri**
This system is made up of three stars, the closest of which is called Proxima Centauri.
4.24-4.37 ly

What is a light year?

This is the distance light travels in one year. Light travels at 300,000 km a second (about 7.5 times around Earth).

7.5

That's equivalent to 9,460,528,400,000 km in a whole year!

Ross 248

8

This is a single, small, dim red star.

10.32 ly

Types of star

Astronomers classify stars in spectral types, depending on their colour, make-up and the temperature at which they burn. Each type is given a letter.

O — O-class stars are blue and have a temperature of up to 50,000°C.

B — B-class stars are blue-white and have a temperature of up to 28,000°C.

A — A-class stars are white and have a temperature of up to 10,000°C.

F — F-class stars are pale yellow and have a temperature of up to 7,500°C.

G — G-class stars, such as our Sun, are yellow and have a temperature of up to 6,000°C.

K — K-class stars are orange and have a temperature of up to 4,900°C

M — M-class stars are red and have a temperature of up to 3,500°C.

Barnard's Star

2

This small star is very dim and is not visible to the naked eye from Earth.

5.96 ly

Luyten 726

6

This system is made up of two small red stars that are slowly orbiting each other.

8–8.73 ly

Ross 154

7

This is a single red star.

9.68 ly

Lacille 9352

10

Even though this is a red star, it is quite bright and can be seen using binoculars.

10.74 ly

INTO SPACE

Humans have been exploring space for over 50 years, using robots or sending people. Launched in 1977, the spacecraft Voyager 1 has now travelled over 19 billion km – farther than any other human-made object.

Distance travelled by extraterrestrial rovers

Sojourner (Mars) – 0.1 km
This small rover was active on the Martian surface from July to September 1997.

Robot rovers have proved extremely useful in exploring other bodies in the Solar System. Many have lasted well beyond their scheduled mission, sending back vital information.

Spirit (Mars) – 7.7 km
This rover was active from 2004 until it became stuck in the Martian soil and lost contact in 2010.

Curiosity (Mars) – 8.6 km
Landing on Mars in 2012, Curiosity is about the size of a small car.

Lunokhod 1 (Moon) – 10.5 km
This Soviet craft was the first robot rover to explore another object in the Solar System. It operated from November 1970 to September 1971.

Eugene Cernan drove the Apollo 17 lunar rover to 17 km/h, setting a speed record for extraterrestrial rovers.

Moon rock

Between 1969 and 1972, the Apollo missions brought back **382 kg** of lunar rock samples – more than the weight of **five people**.

LONGEST HUMAN SPACE FLIGHTS

1. **Valeri Polyakov (Russia) 437.7 days (1994–5)**

2. **Sergei Avdeyev (Russia) 379.6 days (1998–9)**

3. **Vladimir Titov and Musa Manarov (USSR) 365.0 days (1987–8)**

4. **Yuri Romanenko (USSR) 326.5 days (1987)**

5. **Sergei Krikalev (USSR/Russia) 311.8 days (1991–2)**

6. **Valeri Polyakov (USSR) 240.9 days (1988–9)**

7. **Leonid Kizim, Vladimir Solovyov, Oleg Atkov (USSR) 237.0 days (1984)**

8. **Mikhail Tyurin, Michale López-Alegría (Russia, USA) 215.4 days (2006–7)**

9. **Anatoli Berezovoy, Valentin Lebedev (USSR) 211.4 days (1982)**

10. **Talgat Musabayev, Nikolai Budarin (Russia) 207.5 days (1998)**

Animals in Space

Animals sent into space include dogs, cats, chimpanzees, monkeys, spiders, frogs, fish, crickets and ants.

Tiny creatures called tardigrades (water bears) were even exposed to the freezing cold (**-272°C**) of space for 10 days and **survived**!

Apollo 16 rover (Moon) – 27.1 km
Astronauts John Young and Charles Duke drove this rover around the Moon in 1972.

Apollo 15 rover (Moon) – 27.8 km
David Scott and James Irwin used this rover during their three-day stay on the Moon in 1971.

Apollo 17 rover (Moon) – 35.74 km
The last Apollo rover was driven by Eugene Cernan and Harrison Schmitt in 1972.

Lunokhod 2 (Moon) – 39 km
This Soviet lunar rover was active from January to May 1973.

Opportunity (Mars) – 40.25 km
Identical to Spirit, this rover has remained active for more than 10 years.

Food in space

Astronauts' food is precooked or processed so that it does not require refrigeration. Astronauts have 1.7 kg of food to eat a day – the same weight as...

... four cans of soup.

SIZE OF THE UNIVERSE

Space is enormous, which is why distances between stars and galaxies are measured in light years. These images show some of the biggest astronomical bodies in our Solar System, our galaxy, and beyond.

1 Supercluster

These are some of the largest structures in the Universe. The Virgo Supercluster is made up of more than 100 groups of galaxies, called clusters.

110 million ly

2 Galaxy cluster

Galaxies join together to form clusters. The Virgo Cluster contains up to 2,000 galaxies.

5 million ly

3 Galaxy

Stars join together to create galaxies. They can vary greatly in size and shape, but galaxy NGC 6872 is one of the biggest and contains up to 2 trillion stars

522,000 ly

Star cluster

4 Within galaxies, stars move about in groups called clusters. One of the biggest in our galaxy is a globular cluster called Omega Centauri.

230 ly

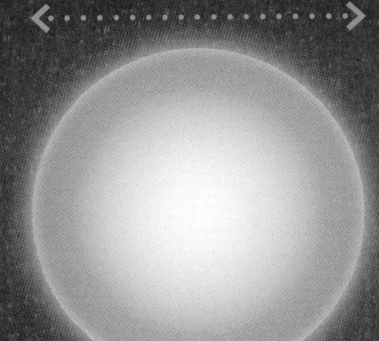

Star

5 One of the largest stars in our galaxy is VY Canis Majoris. It is more than 2,000 times the size of our Sun.

1.4 billion km

Planet

6 Jupiter is the largest planet in our Solar System. It is a huge ball of gas with a solid core.

142,984 km

Dwarf planet

7 Ceres is one of the largest dwarf planets in our Solar System. It orbits the Sun in an area called the Asteroid Belt.

950 km

Moon

8 Moons are natural satellites that orbit around planets. The largest in our Solar System is Ganymede.

5,268 km

Asteroid

9 The Asteroid Belt lies between Mars and Jupiter and contains millions of rocks. The largest of these asteroids is Pallas.

545 km

Comet

10 A comet's nucleus is a 'dirty snowball' of ice and dust. Comet Hale-Bopp has the largest known nucleus.

100 km

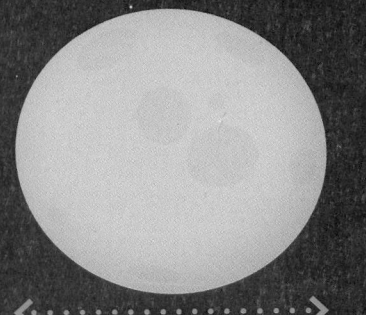

GLOSSARY

acid rain
Rain with a high concentration of harmful, poisonous chemicals that can cause the rain to act like an acid, eroding things it lands on.

asteroid
A large rock that orbits the Sun. Asteroids are smaller than planets and are usually irregularly shaped, rather than spherical.

axial tilt
The amount by which a planet is tilted on its axis – the imaginary line running vertically through its centre.

carbon dioxide
A colourless, odourless gas present in the atmosphere. Animals, including humans, breathe in oxygen and breathe out carbon dioxide. Plants absorb carbon dioxide during photosynthesis.

circumference
The distance around the edge of a circle or curved shape.

comet
A small body made of ice and dust that travels in a long, stretched-out orbit around the Sun. Comets heat up and begin to break apart near the Sun, forming long tails of dust and gas.

desert
An area of the Earth that receives very little rainfall and supports little or no vegetation. Deserts can be hot or cold.

diameter
The width of a circle or sphere measured through its centre point.

dwarf planet
A body in our Solar System that is spherically shaped, but not large enough to be considered a true planet.

exoplanet
A planet that orbits a star outside of our Solar System.

globular cluster
A large, dense ball of stars that orbits around the centre of a galaxy.

light year
A unit of measurement equal to the distance light travels in a year: around 9.6 trillion kilometres.

mass
The amount of matter in a body or bodies, measured in kilograms.

orbit
The path a body takes as it travels around another body, such as the Moon travelling around Earth, or Earth travelling around the Sun.

oxygen
Making up around 20 per cent of Earth's atmosphere, oxygen is a colourless, odourless gas. Plants produce oxygen, and absorb carbon dioxide during photosynthesis.

photosynthesis
The process via which plants use the energy from sunlight to convert carbon dioxide and water from the ground into food, and produce oxygen as a waste product.

rain shadow
A region on one side of a mountainous area that remains dry because the mountains prevent the rain from reaching it.

rover
A vehicle used to explore the surface of another planet or body. It can be manned or unmanned.

shooting star
A streak of light across the night sky, usually formed when a small piece of rock from an asteroid or a comet burns up in Earth's atmosphere.

Solar System
The Sun plus all the objects that orbit it, including planets, dwarf planets, asteroids and comets.

tectonic plates
The giant pieces of rock that make up Earth's crust.

volume
The amount of physical space taken up by a solid body, liquid or gas. Volume is measured in cubic centimetres.

white dwarf
A small, hot star formed when a larger star collapses in on itself towards the end of its life.

WEBSITES

‹‹ • ››

MORE INFO:
http://www.nasa.gov/audience/forkids/kidsclub/flash/
Lots of facts, games, images and videos from the US space agency.

http://www.guinnessworldrecords.com
The website for all things record-breaking. It is packed with thousands of world records and facts.

http://www.si.edu/Encyclopedia/
The Smithsonian's online encyclopaedia is a great resource for facts about the Earth and Space.

MORE GRAPHICS:
www.visualinformation.info
A website that contains a whole host of infographic material on subjects as diverse as natural history, science, sport and computer games.

www.coolinfographics.com
A collection of infographics and data visualisations from other online resources, magazines and newspapers.

www.dailyinfographic.com
A comprehensive collection of infographics on an enormous range of topics that is updated every day!

INDEX

Acknowledgements

First published in 2015 by Wayland

Copyright © Wayland 2015

Wayland
338 Euston Road
London NW1 3BH

Wayland Australia
Level 17/207 Kent Street
Sydney NSW 2000

All rights reserved.

www.hachette.co.uk

Series editor: Julia Adams

Produced by Tall Tree Ltd
Editor: Jon Richards
Designer: Ed Simkins

Dewey classification: 523-dc23

ISBN: 9780750287517
ebook ISBN: 9780750287487

Printed in Malaysia
Wayland is a division of Hachette
Children's Books, an Hachette UK
company.

The website addresses (URLs) included in this book were valid at the time of going to press. However, because of the nature of the Internet, it is possible that some addresses may have changed, or sites may have changed or closed down, since publication. While the author and Publisher regret any inconvenience this may cause the readers, no responsibility for any such changes can be accepted by either the author or the Publisher.

GET THE PICTURE!

Welcome to the world of visual learning! Icons, pictograms and infographics present information in a new and appealing way.

the world in infographics
PLANET EARTH
9780750278461

the world in infographics
SPACE
9780750278454

the world in infographics
COUNTRIES
9780750283069

the world in infographics
MACHINES AND VEHICLES
9780750281287

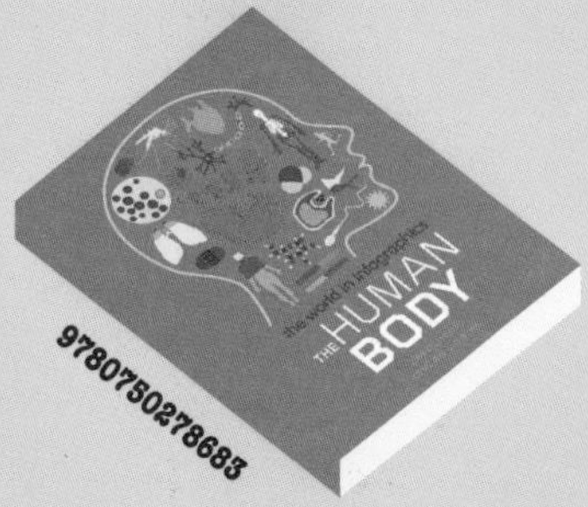

the world in infographics
THE HUMAN BODY
9780750278685

the world in infographics
NATURAL RESOURCES
9780750283205

the world in infographics
THE HUMAN WORLD
9780750269049

the world in infographics
ANIMAL KINGDOM
9780750283199

the world in infographics
SPORT
9780750277792

the world in infographics
THE NATURAL WORLD
9780750269052

the world in infographics
ART AND ENTERTAINMENT
9780750279628

the world in infographics
TECHNOLOGY
9780750285076

go figure
[A Maths] JOURNEY through
SPACE
Exciting and fun numb3r challenges
9780750282390

go figure
[A Maths] JOURNEY through the
Animal Kingdom
Exciting and fun numb3r challenges
9780750282406

go figure
[A Maths] JOURNEY through the
Human Body
Exciting and fun numb3r challenges
9780750282413

go figure
[A Maths] JOURNEY around
Planet Earth
Exciting and fun numb3r challenges
9780750282420